Mama

Harrison Nowotny

Presentation by *BookLeaf Publishing*

Web: www.bookleafpub.com

E-mail: info@bookleafpub.com

ISBN: 9789357440271

First edition 2023

DEDICATION

To Mama. To my sister. To Diya.

ACKNOWLEDGEMENT

This wouldn't have happened without my girlfriend's constant encouragement and support. She never let me believe, for even a second, that I wasn't a good writer. She told me to undertake this challenge, but I never told her that I actually began. I wanted to surprise her, to show her a finished book, and be able to tell her "I did this because of you." Or if it turns out she doesn't like it, be able to say "this is your fault."

And of course, I couldn't have done this without Mama. She is the reason for my love of reading and writing. She was the first to place a book in my hands. The first to place a pencil in one hand and paper in the other. Thank you, Mama. Te amo.

PREFACE

When I made the decision that I wanted to become a writer, I knew my first book had to be about Mama. She is the single most influential person in my life and I wouldn't be where I am now, much less anywhere, without her. This book is a message to my family, my friends, to show them the hardship that their kindness brought me through. To show them that their love wasn't wasted on me.

This book is filled with words I could never say. That is why I write.

Mama's Snow Globe

A million brilliant swirling flurries,
Surround a painted monolith,
Mountains grace the horizon,
Their peaks ever reaching,
Ever stretching,
For the stars, the moon, the sun,
Mama constructed a happy place,
Where before she had none,
Evergreen trees populate the foreground,
Branches heavy and burdened with snow,
Where Mama found her happy place,
There was no further place to go,
On her monolith there was a balcony,
So forever there'd be a sight to see,
Of mountains reaching,
Of starlight breaching,
Clouds of snow,
A fairy glow,
She built herself a snow globe:
A house of glass and a cold whisper,
her happy place forever with her.

Alone in a Coffee Shop

In a coffee shop sits a mother and child,
A coffee and a cappuccino,
Alone but for each other,
A foreign child and his mother.
In a land that is not their own,
To everyone they are unknown,
A child that is barely two,
Born in a place he never knew.
In this warm place they could stay awhile,
Mama's eyes reflect his smile,
Whipped cream dances across his lip,
Foam moved by each tiny sip.

Haunt My Dreams

Pressure always haunting my dreams,
The loving glint in your eyes,
Pressure always haunting my dreams,
That love lets me cut ties,
With my stress,
My struggles,
And lies.

Because,
They will always swallow my dreams,
The hatred burning their eyes,
They will always swallow my dreams,
Fire that burnt up the skies,
With an insult,
A match,
In disguise.

But it doesn't matter,
Because,
You said that you'd always love me,
I saw the truth in your eyes,
You said that you'd always love me,
Your love didn't comprise,
Of my tears,
My pain,
My demise.

Rat Tail

Laughter resounded,
As tears welled in my eyes.
They stood above me,
As I lay on the locker room floor.
A whip cracked against a metal door,
The cold floor rebuked me,
No remorse hid behind his smile,
I still remember that smirk.
Lightning struck my side,
Thunder,
Laughter,
Blood,
Pounding in my ears,
I heard the jeers,
The taunts,
The laughter that wouldn't cease,
The whip fell again,
And again,
And again.
I raised my hand above my head,
To try to block the blows,
Until they became bored,
And I was left on the floor,
Alone.

At home Mama made me soup,
She dried my tears,
And held me close,
When no one else would.

The Strongest Person I Know

Mama set aside her career,
To raise us three,
She held my hand near,
Under the old pecan tree,
She whispered in my ear,
Words that would have let me see,
But I couldn't hear,
Tears signified the opposite of ecstasy.

I didn't want cancer to take away Mama.

I wore a shirt for Mama,
Pink with a ribbon,
I swam,
With a hot pink cap,
I swam,
Away the frustration and anger,
I swam,
'Till I felt my heart might explode,
I swam,
And the water hid my tears.

I tried so hard to not let Mama see me cry.

I tried to go to school,
And act like everything was normal,
But my head swirled with emotions,
On the outside I was dead,

Lost to the world,
I just wanted to go home,
To see Mama,
The strongest person I know,
She'd know what to say,
If only now I could listen.

A Different Point of View

Waves come in from the sea,
Yet the waves crash away from me,
I am standing alone,
On sand colored bone,
For sins of time I've atoned,
That's why when I face the shore,
Where I want to be,
Even after seeing the wretched and poor,
Just barely, I can see,
The company I want,
I see her walk away,
Disappear around the corner,
But here I have to stay,
Because I'm stuck in sand,
And frozen by fear,
I couldn't have held her hand,
The ocean catches a tear.
I begin to sink,
Water chokes my vision,
Eyes begin to sting,
They're either tears from missing,
Love or hope.
Thought I was alone in the ocean,
But there are others who mope,
Standing to my left and my right,
Standing together,
But alone they fight,
I can only hope they remember,

Before the last of the light,
Sinks below the horizon,
So much deeper and farther below then I am.

You Will Understand One Day

It always frustrated me to no end,
When Mama told me,
"You'll understand one day",
I couldn't comprehend,
Couldn't understand,
Why I had to study every day,
And always receive an A,
Why when I misbehaved,
She reached for her paddle,
Her shoe,
A belt,
Why I had to hide it if I ever got a welt,
Why I had to go outside,
Every once in a while,
Play in that dusty courtyard,
Rather than inside on the tile,
Never hit your sister,
Or your little brother,
But you can hit for them,
Always family before another,
I never understood this and so much else,
Until one day,
I did.

A Letter to My Sister

When you believe,
There's no one there,
That no one cares,
There's no place for you,
And your all alone,
I'm here for you.

When you feel,
A frigidness you can't explain,
A chill that won't leave,
That you might turn towards the dark,
And fall right in,
I'm here for you.

When you think,
Your friends aren't real,
There's no one you can trust,
Everyone is against you,
That you should probably give up,
I'm here,
With two shoulders to cry on,
Two ears to listen,
Two eyes to share your pain,
And one heart to bear it all.

Don't ever believe that no one loves you,
Because I always will (and so will Dingo),
And I'm only ever one call away.

The Day I Understood

Eyes open,
Veils burn,
Urns spin,
Graves turn,
The day I understood,
The world was born anew,
Washed clean by storm and hellfire,
The ocean boiled then withdrew,
Revealing truth in the seabed,
That if I only I just knew,
Before I said those things,
Those things I didn't mean to you,
But I know that you forgive me,
Those were things that I outgrew,
One day I might just pay you back,
That's a goal I will pursue,
I'll bring it when I come back home,
While the sky's an iridescent blue,
Cause now I understand,
Just how much you have been through,
Having to raise this child,
Couldn't have been an easy thing to do,
But now I'm off to the college,
The end is just beginning to be in view.

For Old Times' Sake

 Screens, Televisions, Phones
"Give him a book," Mama said.
Mama made me read.

Sentences, Books, Worlds
Imagination open
My mind could now see.

Pen, Page, Written word,
Words of mine remain unheard
Waiting for reveal.

Light Ordinance

Darkness falls,
On a town with no lights,
Silence falls,
But for an insect in the night,
But the darkness reveals a million stars,
And the silence unlocks a peace inside.
Stars hidden for some time now,
And a peace some never find.

Día Bonita

A beautiful day,
Filled with blooming flowers,
And rushing creeks,
Cobble roads,
Lined with picturesque boutiques,
A buffet of color,
Each shop is unique,
Just like each blade of grass,
That brushes your skin,
As you lay down and watch the clouds pass,
Again and again,
In the morning pull off the sheets,
To see the morning dew,
A beautiful day is incomplete,
Without you,
You are what makes the day beautiful,
And you are the girl my Mama approves.

A Date at Wal-Mart

Mud tracked into the Wal-Mart on the bottom of his shoes,
Hair all in a frizz and his bills are way past their dues,
Looking lost, like he didn't know which route to choose,
Didn't matter to him, he didn't seem to have much left to lose,
His head down and hung, not taking many cues,
All gray and mud, not many other hues,
All the color in his life then turns the corner,
She wore a green dress and silver on the corners,
Of her eyes,
Eyes that he could get lost in like the night sky,
Eyes that lift him up till he begins to fly,
Wings on his back, lift his head up high,
Still got mud on, whisper him a silly guy,
They walk together among the aisles,
He would follow her to the British Isles,
Just a beautiful smile,
And a muddy exile.

Un Verano Sin Ti

Can't imagine,
Un verano sin ti,
If you weren't in my life,
I can't fathom who'd be,
You mean as much to me,
As Un Verano Sin Ti,
Music changed my life,
I think my soul would agree,
You found me,
When I was still lost out at sea,
Raging foam and waves,
Could have brought tragedy,
But I bleed,
Words onto paper and tears into a sea,
Turn pain and trauma,
Into a story you can read,
Bad trips and drama,
Are webs that I weave,
Into stories and characters,
That you could believe,
Just like you believed,
Like you believed in me,
That's why I write for you,
Instead of for me,
A summer without you,
Is like leaves without a tree.

Never Forever Apart

A thousand miles away,
Ten thousand feet above,
A single call a day,
Reminds me of your love.
A message before you go to work,
Means more than you could imagine,
Delivered by a white-feathered stork,
Your word a miracle I can barely fathom.

Yet it brings me joy beyond compare,
And a smile I wish I could share,
But for a thousand miles between us,
On distance is where I place the blame,
Physically so far above,
The air we breathe is not the same,
Yet you are still with me in my mind and heart,
You always will be,
Never forever apart.

Her Smile's Gone

The day her smile left,
My heart shattered into jagged shards,
That cut and ripped as they exploded outwards,
Tearing apart my will,
And cutting free my hope in this world of ours,
I watched it fly away,
Only as far as the fog would allow me to see,
Lost dreams and agility,
To age and time,
What once was divine,
Is now neither yours,
Nor mine,
Something lost to the ether,
A word landing only upon the wind,
Or a balloon released by an eager hand,
Born away to a forever-lost land,
A land covered in smoke and amnesia,
Forgotten by all who had seen her,
It may be a while,
Until I see her smile flash once again,
And my shattered heart begins to mend.

Preschool Mafia

Connections with the mob got me into pre-K4,
Same type of guys who'll kick down your door,
And decorate your floor,
Just to settle a score,
Get the blood out your rug,
Then send your kid to school,
I didn't speak the language,
So I came up with a rule,
Watch my back at nap time,
And mop up my drool,
If we share food at snack time,
Then I know that we're cool,
Made a friend with a kid in a spider-man shirt,
Shared part of his apple,
And he showed me how to flirt,
With the girls in Italian,
Didn't know what I was saying,
But I was sure I was styling,
A little four-year-old with barely a grasp of his feet,
Don't know how I expected to get one of those girl's deets,
That's why at lunch I ended up sitting all on my own,
Just waiting for my Mama to come take me home,
I felt a tear drop,
Into my bowl of Mac and Cheese,
When I finally saw Mama,
I'd never been so pleased.

Mama's Laugh

I could always make Mama laugh,
She called me the funny one, her comedian,
Her sunshine,
She also called me Kramer,
Because I was (and still am) very clumsy,
And would fall,
All,
The,
Damn,
Time.
But if no one else was getting my joke,
I could always count on her to laugh,
Possibly because we shared a sense of humor,
Or she had passed her humor on to me,
Introducing humorists such as Abbot and Castello to me,
At a very young age,
While my father believed someone injuring themselves,
Was the funniest thing that could happen,
Mama understood my sarcasm,
My wit,
My deadpan delivery,
And I never cared if nobody laughed,
As long as I saw her smile,
With that sparkle in her eye.

New Year's Resolution

I resolve to be a better person,
To eat healthier,
To work out more,
To drink more water,
To get up early,
To be more social,
To use less social media,
To be a better brother,
A better boyfriend,
A better son,
To do a hundred push-ups a day,
No, two hundred a day,
To write more,
To join a volunteer organization,
To produce and sell a beat,
To try-out for a play,
To have a small speaking role,
To get an agent,
To start my own volunteer organization,
To invent something new,
To get published in a magazine,
To start my own business,
To appear on Shark Tank,
To write a book and get it published,
To write and sell a screenplay,
To be part of a supporting cast,
To star in an action movie,
To produce my own album,

To make it on the billboard hot one hundred,
To become a superstar with a million adoring fans,
To eliminate world hunger,
To lift everyone from poverty,
To reverse climate change,
To broker peace between every nation in the world,

And…

Stop expecting so much of myself.

To Be a Writer

I wrote a poem,
It wasn't good,
So I wrote another,
It wasn't bad,
So I kept on writing,
They told me the only way to become a better writer,
Was to write,
So I wrote,
Day after day,
After day,
Page after page,
After page,
Two hundred and sixty-two days later,
I am still writing,
I don't plan on stopping,
Because now I spend every day,
Working towards a goal,
An objective,
A destination,
An ambition,
A dream,
That I move on hands and knees towards,
And yet still I crawl,
Because I was raised by my Mama,
And told that when I fall,
Draw back the hammer,
And stand up tall.

A Letter to Mama

Mama, when you told me to always be kind,
I listened,
When you told me to always work hard,
I worked,
When you told me life was hard,
I worked harder,
When you told me that I have to believe in myself,
I remembered.

Mama, when you told me I was smart,
You were the only one I believed,
When you told me I could be anything I wanted,
I looked to the heavens,
When you told me to follow my passion,
I wrote down my dreams,
When you told me you'd never leave me,
I believed you.

When I told you I wanted to be a writer,
You smiled, but you did not laugh,
When I told you that one day I will buy you a car, a house,
You said you already had everything you wanted,
When I told you that one day I would pay you back,
You said that I already did,
When I told you I'd never give up,
I did not lie.

When you told me you loved me,
I loved you too,
And I always will,
Mama.